To Emily, our first grandchild.
Jesus is a friend for every day.
N.R.

Everyday Prayers

for Children

LOIS ROCK

ST. ANTHONY MESSENGER PRESS

Cincinnati, Ohio

Text copyright ©2001, Lois Rock. Original edition published in
English under the title *The Lion Book of Everyday Prayers for
Children* by Lion Publishing plc, Oxford, England.
Copyright ©2001 Lion Publishing plc
ISBN 0 7459 4702 6

A catalogue record for this book is available from the British Library.

Published and distributed in the United States of America and Canada
by St. Anthony Messenger Press
28 W. Liberty Street
Cincinnati, OH 45210
www.AmericanCatholic.org

  Library of Congress Cataloging-in-Publication Data

Rock, Lois, 1953-
    [Lion book of everyday prayers for children]
    Everyday prayers for children / Lois Rock.
      p. cm.
    Previously published as: The Lion book of everyday prayers for
children.
    Includes index.
    Summary: A collection of all kinds of prayers arranged in such
groupings as: Beginnings, My World, Great and Wonderful, Faith,
and Through the Night.
    ISBN 0-86716-501-4
    1. Children–Prayer-books and devotions–English.   [1. Prayers.]

  I. Title.
  BV212.R625 2002
  242'.82–dc21

    2002002146

ISBN 0-86716-501-4

Printed in Singapore.

Contents

ABOUT PRAYER

It is an old custom of the servants of God to have some little prayers ready to hand, and to be frequently darting them up to heaven during the day.

Philip Neri

A way to start

I offer to God a simple prayer
That I hardly know how to start.
It has grown by itself from somewhere deep
In the treasures of my heart.

Inspired by Francois de Knuyt (1618)

Don't worry about anything, but in all your prayers ask God for what you need, always asking him with a thankful heart.

Philippians 4:6

A low prayer, a high prayer, I send through space.
Arrange them Thyself, O thou King of Grace.

From The Poem-Book of the Gael

Lord, you know what I want.
If you think it right, may I have it.
If you do not think it right,
good Lord, do not be displeased that I asked,
for I don't want anything that you don't want.

After Julian of Norwich (1342–c. 1416)

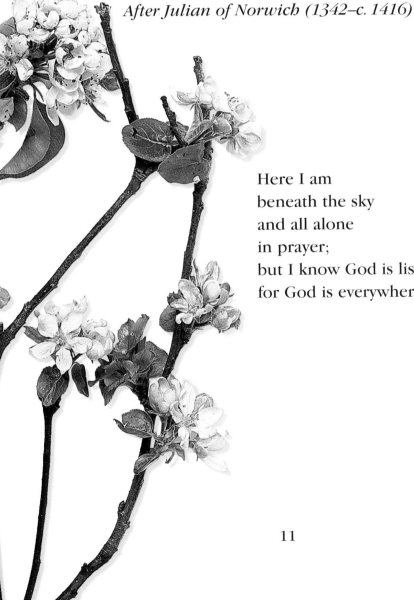

Here I am
beneath the sky
and all alone
in prayer;
but I know God is listening,
for God is everywhere.

2

BEGINNINGS

Every day is a new beginning,
Hark, my soul, to the glad refrain,
And, spite of old sorrow and older sinning,
Trouble forecasted and possible pain,
Take heart with the day and begin again.

Unknown

Morning

Thank you, God in heaven,
For a day begun.
Thank you for the breezes,
Thank you for the sun.
For this time of gladness,
For our work and play,
Thank you, God in heaven,
For another day.

Traditional

Through the night Thy angels kept
Watch above me while I slept,
Now the dark has passed away,
Thank Thee, Lord, for this new day.

William Canton

O sweet and loving God,
When I stay asleep too
    long,
Dreamily unaware of all the
    good things you do for me,
Please wake me up to know
    that you are there
With a song that sings to
    my soul.

*After Mechthild of
Magdeburg (c. 1210–80)*

Come into my soul, Lord,
as the dawn breaks into the sky;
let your sun rise in my heart
at the coming of the day.

Traditional

Remind me each morning of your constant love,
for I put my trust in you.

Psalm 143:8

15

The day ahead

Dear God,
Sometimes I wake to a day that is calm and bright.
Help me to discover its fun and delight.
Sometimes I wake to a day that is cloudy with
    threatening storms.
Help me to brave it with courage and cheerfulness.

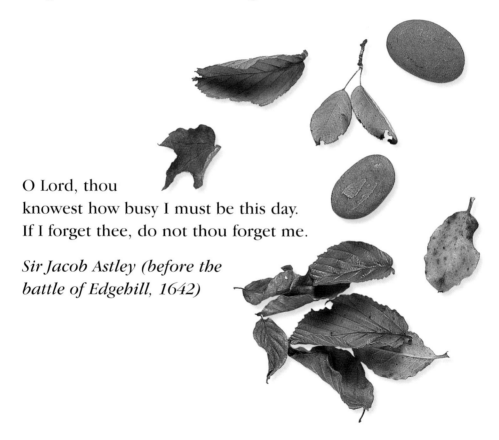

O Lord, thou
knowest how busy I must be this day.
If I forget thee, do not thou forget me.

*Sir Jacob Astley (before the
battle of Edgehill, 1642)*

I go forth today
in the might of heaven,
in the brightness of the
    sun,
in the whiteness of
    snow,
in the splendour of fire,
in the speed of lightning,
in the swiftness of wind,
in the firmness of rock.
I go forth today
in the hand of God.

Eighth-century
Irish prayer

Good resolutions

I shall pass through this world but once.
Any good therefore that I can do
    or any kindness that I can show
        to any human being
           let me do it now.

              Let me not defer
              or neglect it,
              for I shall not
              pass this way
              again.

            Anonymous

Quietly, in the morning,
I rise and look at the sky
To watch the darkness scatter
As sunlight opens the sky.
The day lies clear before me,
All fresh and shining and new,
And then I ask God to guide me
In all that I have to do.

Walk the way of kindness,
Walk the way of right;
Walk the way of wisdom,
Walk the way of light.

God be in the little things
    of all I do today
So at the end the whole
    may be
    perfect in every way.

Let this day, O Lord, add
some knowledge or
good deed to yesterday.

*Lancelot Andrewes
(1555–1626)*

19

The way of kindness

Lord, make us to walk in your way:
'Where there is love and wisdom, there is neither
fear nor ignorance;
where there is patience and humility, there is
neither anger nor annoyance;
where there is poverty and joy, there is
neither greed nor avarice;
where there is peace and contemplation,
there is neither care nor restlessness;
where there is the fear of God to guard the
dwelling, there no enemy can enter;
where there is mercy and prudence, there is neither
excess nor harshness';
this we know through your Son, Jesus Christ
our Lord.

Francis of Assisi (1181–1226)

I think of those I hate to love
and those I love to hate:
help us accept our differences
before it is too late.

The things, good Lord, that we pray for,
give us grace to work for; through
Jesus Christ our Lord.

Thomas More (1478–1535)

We can do no great things,
Only small things with great love.

Mother Teresa of Calcutta (1910–97)

Where there is no love, put love, and you will
receive love back.

St John of the Cross (1542–91)

O God,
Fill the quiet spaces
in my life with love.

Guide my way

You are my God;
teach me to do your will.
Be good to me, and guide me on a safe path.

Psalm 143:10

Guide me in my growing older,
Wiser, gentler,
Braver, bolder.

O God, help us not to despise or oppose
what we do not understand.

William Penn (1644–1718)

Dearest Lord, teach me to be generous;
Teach me to serve you as you deserve;
To give and not to count the cost,
To fight and not to heed the wounds,
To toil and not to seek for rest,
To labour and not to seek reward,
Save that of knowing that I do your will.

Ignatius Loyola (1491–1556)

I travel this world by sunlight,
seeing the way I should go;
I travel this world by moonlight,
trusting its silvery glow;
I travel this world by starlight,
trusting in heaven above;
I walk through this old world's darkness,
safe in the light of God's love.

3

MY WORLD

Dear God,
Ferry me safely across the sea of life:
its calms, its storms,
its shallows, its deeps,
its familiar shoreline and its far horizon.

Me

Dear Father, who hast all things made,
And carest for them all,
There's none too great for thy great love,
Nor anything too small;
If thou canst spend such tender care
On things that grow so wild,
How wonderful thy love must be
For me, thy little child.

G.W. Briggs (1875–1959)

I can't be everybody and I can't be
everywhere,
I know I'm not just anyone, just wandering
anywhere;
I sometimes feel like nobody, with no place
of my own,
Please let me be a somebody, with
somewhere that's my home.

A small child on earth
Needs a big God in heaven
And angels to help run messages.

Write my name on the palm
  of your hand,
Remember me all my days.
Write my name in the book
  of heaven
And keep me safe always.

Though I may be small,
I know I am big in your eyes,
Lord.

A child's prayer

Thank you for the year gone by
and all that I have done.
Thank you for my birthday
and the year that is to come.

These are mine

Dear God,
Thank you for cuddly toys,
for their bright smiles
and warm hugs
that help us learn to love
and to be loved.

Thank you for new shoes,
new places to go
and new beginnings.

Dear God,
Help us to enjoy things we have that are new.
Help us to use them until they are old.
Help us to say goodbye to them,
and to remember the happy times we had together.

If I had a million of money
And could buy me a million things
I'd wish for to buy me a million years
And all of the fun they could bring.

But money can't buy me a minute
And to me it no longer seems odd
That people care less about money
Than to walk hand in hand with their God.

Working days

With God you must let things begin,
With God let all things come to rest;
In this way the work of your hands
Will flourish and also be blessed.

From an old bookplate

Oh, you gotta get a glory
In the work you do;
A Hallelujah chorus
In the heart of you.
Paint, or tell a story,
Sing, or shovel coal,
But you gotta get a glory,
Or the job lacks soul.

Anonymous

Bless to me, O Lord,
the work of my hands.
Bless to me, O God,
the work of my mind.
Bless to me, O God,
the work of my heart.

Anonymous

Eternal Father, strong to save,
my computer's crashed.
Please may I find the work I did –
may it not be trashed.

Let the favour of the Lord our God be upon us,
and prosper for us the work of our hands –
O prosper the work of our hands!

Psalm 90:17

Free time

Time to dream,
time to think,
time to be young,
time to grow old.
Time to be still while the world turns round.
Time to grow wise while there is still time.

Dear God,
Thank you for time I can spend
doing nothing much.

God of all the
hours there are,
We humbly pray to thee:
Bring some good from all the time
We spend at the TV.

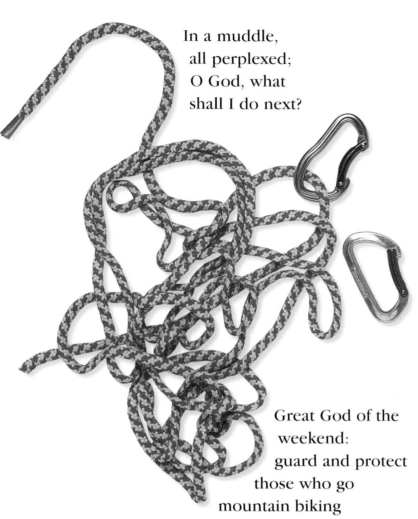

In a muddle,
   all perplexed;
   O God, what
   shall I do next?

Great God of the
   weekend:
   guard and protect
   those who go
   mountain biking
moorland hiking
scuba diving
paragliding
rollerblading
cliff abseiling
bungee jumping
river running…
Bring them home safe.
Bring them all home.

Holidays

With God, nothing is impossible.
Dear God,
As you plan the weather for the holidays,
please bear in mind the needs of
swimmers,
surfers,
kite flyers,
walkers,
cyclists,
campers…
Whilst not forgetting
gardeners,
farmers,
ducks
and those who do not have holidays.
With God, nothing is impossible.

Dear God,
Be good to me,
The sea is so wide
And my boat is so small.

Prayer of Breton fishermen

Let us give thanks for holidays:
for swimsuits and towels
sandals and sunglasses
cold drinks and ice-cream
racquets, balls, kites
maps, tickets, postcards
new places to see
new places to stay
and God watching over us
wherever we may go.

May this holiday
Be a jolly day.

Journeys

Father, lead us through this day
As we travel on our way
Be our safety, be our friend
Bring us to our journey's end.
I take the bus to the great unknown
Dear God, don't let me feel alone.
I take the train, and I go so far –
Dear God, do you know where we are?
I take the plane to a distant shore
Dear God, I hope you've been before.

My journey may be fast or
My journey may be slow;
May God be always with me
Wherever I may go.

Heavenly Father,
As we journey
Keep us safe
Keep us brave
Keep us going.

The Lord will protect you from all danger;
he will keep you safe.
He will protect you as you come and go
now and for ever.

Psalm 121:7–8

Mothers and fathers and those who take care of us

Dear God,
I pray for my mother:
May she know when to work and when to stop,
When to get angry and when to stay calm,
When to tidy up and when to let things go,
When to splash out and when to be thrifty,
And help her to make up her own mind
About when she wants dessert.

Bless my mum –
she is the best –
with busy days
and nights of rest.

Dear God,
I think of my dad and offer
Thanking prayers...
Grumbling prayers...
Cheerful prayers...
Grumpy prayers...
And always, always, lots of prayers
To keep him safe and good.

Sometimes my dad makes me feel so proud
and sometimes I just want to hide,
And I think that my dad, who's so strong and so tall,
is a bit of a kid deep inside.

Dear God,
I pray for those who take care of me as I grow up.
Please help and encourage them, and may you always
be to me the Grandest, Greatest Parent of them all.

The wider family

Here is our baby from heaven
who must have come down on a cloud
so little, so soft and so pretty
and also amazingly loud.

For all the times we've
loved and laughed
And fought and rowed and hated
We give a cautious thanks for those
To whom we are related.

Brothers and sisters need to be close
and to have their own space.

Dear God,
Help me to remember always the things that my
grandparents tell me – their stories, their sayings,
their songs.

Dear God,
We think of all those who have become family to us.
May we grow to love and understand each other more
and more.

God bless all those that I love;
God bless all those that love me;
God bless all those that love those that I love
and all those that love those that love me.

New England sampler

Home

Father of all mankind, make the roof of my house wide
enough for all opinions, oil the door of my house so it
opens easily to friend and
stranger, and set such a table
in my house that my whole
family may speak kindly and
freely around it. Amen.

Prayer from Hawaii

Bless this house which is our home
May we welcome all who come.

Anonymous

Dear God,
Fill our home with
beautiful things:
Kind words
Warm welcomes
Fond goodbyes
Happy chatter
Easy silence
Togetherness
Space
Love.

Bless our home, Father,
that we cherish the bread before there is none,
discover each other before we leave,
and enjoy each other for what we are,
while we have time.

Anonymous (Hawaiian)

Food

Each time we eat,
May we remember God's love.

Chinese grace

Heavenly Father, great and holy
Help me eat this fast food slowly.

Food is good and food is fun:
thank you for this lunch for one.

For health and strength
and daily food,
we praise your name,
O Lord.

Traditional

44

The bread is warm and fresh,
The water cool and clear.
Lord of all life, be with us,
Lord of all life, be near.

African grace

Bread is a lovely thing to eat –
God bless the barley and the wheat!

A lovely thing to breathe is air –
God bless the sunshine everywhere!

The earth's a lovely place to know –
God bless the folks that come and go!

Alive's a lovely thing to be –
Giver of life – we say – bless Thee!

H.M. Sarson

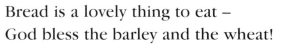

Friends

Let our friendships be strong, O Lord,
that they become a blessing to others…
Let our friendships be open, O Lord,
that they may be a haven for others…
Let our friendships be gentle, O Lord,
that they may bring peace to others…
for Jesus' sake. Amen.

Christopher Herbert

Dear God,
 Thank you for friends –
  for secrets and projects and laughter
and sympathy;
     for times of dreaming and
      planning;
        for hours spent
         remembering;
         for mistakes and
         forgiveness and for not
       remembering;
        for yesterday, today and
         tomorrow.

Thank you for friends.
Dear God,
May we sit down with friends
    through all our days:
On the plastic chairs
    of playgroup,
On the wooden chairs
    at school,
On the soft and sagging sofas
    of home,
On the folding chairs
    of holidays,
On the fashionable seats
    of restaurants
And on the dusty seats
    in the garden
Till at last, when we have
    grown old, we need our
    friends to help us in and
    out of chairs.

Gentle love for babies.
Enduring love for family.
Patient love for friends.
Resolute love for enemies.
Everlasting love from God.

Not friends

Dear God,
Do you know how disappointing
friends can sometimes be?

A true friend can keep a secret;
But what's the secret of keeping a true friend?

Dear God,
I sometimes feel I have no friends.
Let me know you listen to me
so I do not feel alone.

Dear God,
I pray for people who spoil
the day with rudeness and
cheating and nastiness. Help
me to survive them. Help
them to change their ways.

Enemies are awful
and enemies are mean
but all their wicked, wicked deeds
by God above are seen.
Now God is all forgiving
but God is also good
and God will sort them out one day
just like I wish I could.

Dear God,
I have noticed just how often friends let me down.
They don't come along to do the things they said they'd do,
nor do they say the things they promised to say.
Help me to get on with the day without them,
and to bring from it something different, something good.

Animal friends

Dear God,
My cat is more lovely than a lion,
more perfect than a panther,
more terrifying than a tiger,
more charming than a cheetah
and more strokeable than a stick insect!
Thank you for my cat.

Dear God,
Please teach
me how to
follow you
and teach my
dog how to
follow me.

Dear God,
My friends have such terrifying pets. Please help
me to be brave when I am supposed to show how
much I like them.

Give thanks to God for the goldfish
Who swims round and round in a bowl
While the dream of an ocean-filled heaven
Still stirs in his fishy-sized soul.

For the gentle, wide-eyed
animals who love us, we give
you thanks, O God.

51

School

Dear God,
We return to school from the freedom of the holidays.
The outlook is bleak, for we have forgotten the
routine of the school day and a good bit of what
we learned last year.
Dear God, we pray for survival.

Dear God,
Save us from lessons that are like a grey fog.
Grant us lessons of summer blue,
and the golden sunlight of inspiration.

Dear God,
    When I don't know the right answer,
    please help me ask the right
    question.

    May angels guard all our belongings,
    may angels guard all of our work
    from thieves and from louts and
        from bullies
    who out in the corridors lurk.

Dear God,
Help our teachers to be strict and fair and kind and funny.

Dear God,
Help me to look forward to each school day,
hoping to make discoveries;
help me to look back on every school day,
pleased with what I have learned and understood.

4

THE WIDER WORLD

Dear God,
Bring us all to a place of safety
in an uncertain world.

People of the world

Bless our beautiful land, O Lord,
with its wonderful variety of people,
of races, cultures and languages.
May we be a nation
of laughter and joy,
of justice and reconciliation,
of peace and unity,
of compassion, caring and sharing.
We pray this prayer for a true patriotism,
in the powerful name of Jesus our Lord.

Desmond Tutu

Pour forth,
O Christ,
your love
upon this land
today.

Anonymous

We welcome all the birds that fly to us
   from other lands.
   Let's welcome other people and reach out
   to hold their hands.

Grandfather, look at our brokenness.
   We know that in all creation only the
   human family has strayed from the sacred way.
We know that we are the ones who are divided
and we are the ones who must come back
together to walk in the sacred way.
Grandfather, Sacred One,
teach us love, compassion and honour
that we may heal the earth and each other.

Native American prayer, World Council of Churches

Young and old

Think about the generations:
children, bright and energetic like spring;
the just-grown-ups like summer
and the mums and dads like harvest time
mellowing into autumn;
then the granny generation with frost in their hair;
and the very old like winter
and the light from heaven
that lights our way through all our days.

I think of the
generations
of my family
through all the
years of time.
I think of how
each generation
has hoped that the children will grow up well.

May I, who am the child of them all,
keep faith with God and with myself,
and keep their hope alive.

Individuals

I'm not as swift as a cheetah,
Nor quick to hear like a bat,
Nor sharp of sight like an eagle,
Yet you love me in spite of all that.

There are activities in
which we can take part.
There are activities
when we have to sit
on the sidelines.
Help us to play all
our parts well,
and to cheer from
the sidelines.

They tell me that everyone's special,
As special to God as can be,
But inside I just feel normal –
Is everyone special but me?

We think about the ways in which we are like others.
We think about the ways in which we are unlike others.
We think about the ways in which we can help the world,
and the ways in which we need to be helped.

People in need

There's trouble in the fields, Lord,
The crops are parched and dry.
We water them with tears, Lord,
So help us, hear our cry.

There's trouble in our hearts, Lord,
The world is full of pain.
Set us to work for healing,
Send blessings down like rain.

We pray, mighty God,
for those who struggle
that their life's flickering
flame may not be
snuffed out.
We pray for the poor
and deprived, for those
exploited by the powerful
and greedy, and for a
more human sharing of
the plenty you have given
your world.

Prayer from India

To live truly and openly,
without riches or poverty,
without fear or superstition,
without lies,
without malice,
with a heart open to goodness:
to truly live.

Lord of the wild earth,
    of the boiling rocks and the raging storms,
    mark out a boundary for the tempest,
    and make for all your people a garden home
    where we can gather our harvests
and celebrate your goodness.

War

In the muddy fields of war, may
we scatter the seeds of peace.

Lord, make
me an
instrument
of your
peace.
Where there
   is hatred, let me sow love;
Where there is injury, pardon;
Where there is discord, union;
Where there is doubt, faith;
Where there is despair, hope;
Where there is darkness, light;
Where there is sadness, joy.

O divine Master, grant that I may not
so much seek to be consoled, as to console,
to be understood, as to understand, to be loved,
as to love; for it is in giving that we receive,
it is in pardoning that we are pardoned,
and it is in dying that we are born to eternal life.

Attributed to St Francis of Assisi (1181–1226)

Dear God,
Give us the courage
to overcome anger
with love.

Shield us from violence,
Shield us from harm,
Find for us a shelter
Of quiet and of calm.

O Brother Jesus, who as a child
    was carried into exile,
Remember all those who are
    deprived of their home or
        country,
Who groan under the burden
    of anguish and sorrow,
Enduring the burning heat of the sun,
The freezing cold of the sea, or the humid heat of the
    forest,
Searching for a place of refuge.
Cause these storms to cease,
    O Christ.
Move the hearts of those in power
That they may respect the men
    and women
Whom you have created in your own image;
That the grief of refugees may be turned into joy.

Prayer from Africa

65

Tolerance

My Father in heaven, I remember those
whom in prayer I am inclined to forget.
I pray for those whom I dislike.
Defend me against my own feelings;
change my inclinations;
give me a compassionate heart.
Give me, I pray, the purity of heart
which finds your image in all people.

J.H. Jowett (1846–1923)

O Great Spirit, help me never to judge
another until I have walked two
weeks in his moccasins.

*Prayer of the Sioux
Indians*

Love is giving, not taking,
mending, not breaking,
trusting, believing,
never deceiving,
patiently bearing
and faithfully sharing
each joy, every sorrow,
today and tomorrow.

Anonymous

Thank you, dear God,
for the blessing of things that stay
    the same:
for people we have known for ever
and the familiar paths where
    we walk.

Thank you, dear God,
for the blessing of things that
    change:
for newcomers with their new
    customs,
new ways of doing things, new
    paths to discover.

Thank you, dear God,
for the blessing of the old and the blessing of the new.

5

GREAT AND WONDERFUL WORLD

Here on the ancient rock of earth
I sit and watch the sky;
I feel the breeze that moves the trees
While stately clouds float by.
I wonder why our planet home
Spins round and round the sun
And what will last for ever
When earth's days all are done.

Creation

Our God is the God of all,
The God of heaven and earth,
Of the sea and the rivers;
The God of the sun and of the moon
   and of all the stars;
The God of the lofty mountains
   and of the lowly valleys,
He has His dwelling around heaven
   and earth, and sea, and all that in them is.

St Patrick (c. 389–c. 461)

Glory to God for everything!

John Chrysostom (c. 347–407)

All things praise thee Lord most high!
Heaven and earth and sea and sky!

Time and space are praising thee!
All things praise thee; Lord, may we!

George William Condor (1821–74)

All things bright and beautiful,
All creatures great and small,
  All things wise and wonderful,
   The Lord God
   made them all.

*Mrs C.F. Alexander
(1818–95)*

The world and all that is
in it belong to the Lord;
the earth and all who
live on it are his.

Psalm 24:1

71

Landscapes

Great and wonderful world
lit with gold and silver
furnished all in green
and newly colourwashed each day
in sky shades of blue and grey,
lavender, violet and flame:
the Great Maker of all the world
requires that I should take care of you
and that you should take care of me.

We praise you, O Maker, for rushing rivers that bring
the joy of the mountains into the valleys.
We praise you for slow rivers, eddying into quiet pools
where we can sit and rest.
We praise you for the great sea, in which all rivers meet
and are lifted up to heaven.

I love to be down by the sea,
  watching the shifting tide
    and the changing boundaries
     of land and water
      and dreaming of the day
       when heaven itself
        will break like a silver wave
         on the dust of earth.

A city is a temple of the material world
With buildings of brick and concrete, steel and glass,
Interlinking highways, secret alleyways,
An underground network of pipes and tunnels,
An overhead tangle of wires and airwaves.
But it rests in the lap of the patient earth
Under the gentle gaze of a sky that reaches to all eternity.
A city is built in a sacred place.

Through the year

I will remember the buds of spring
When summertime leaves are green;

I will remember their rippling shade
When colours of autumn are seen;

I will remember the red and the gold
When wintertime branches are bare;

I will give thanks to the God of the trees
Whose love reaches everywhere.

Harvest time is gold and red:
Thank you for our daily bread.
Christmas time is red and green:
Heaven now on earth is seen.
Easter time is green and white:
Bring us all to heaven's light.

White are the wavetops,
White is the snow:
Great is the One
Who made all things below.

Green are the grasslands,
Green is the tree:
Great is the One
Who has made you and me.

Blue are the cornflowers,
Blue is the sky:
Great is the One
Who made all things on high.

Gold is the harvest,
Gold is the sun:
God is our Maker –
Great is the One.

Seasons

God bless the seeds we scatter
And send the cool grey rain
To mix up with the sunshine
And bring us flowers again.

Thank you, God, for
daffodils. Thank you for their
yellow cheerfulness. Thank you
that they go on dancing
even when the weather is
unkind and nobody bothers
to go outside to admire them.
Thank you for daffodils.

When the skies are blue and gold,
Give us the time to play;
When the skies are grey and cold,
Give us a place to stay.

Thank you for the winter wind that blows;
Thank you for the winter cloud that snows;
Thank you for the scarf around my nose;
Thank you for the socks around my toes.

We thank you, God, for rain: for showers and storms, for downpours and drizzle, and for the grey shifting curtains of water that fill the puddles and the rivers.

Guard our homes from floods, our flowers from flattening, and our umbrellas from collapse.

Remind us of the value of waterproofs, however ugly and unfashionable, and help us to know you are with us, whether we are dry or wet.

Harvests

Dear God,
Guard the sugar harvests:
the cane and the beet, the maple
and the honey.
May the harvesters know the
sweetness of the
crop, and may
they be
rewarded for
their work.
Help us to
appreciate
the many
kinds of
sugar, and
to use them
well.

O God,
You show your care for the
    land by sending rain;
    you make it rich and fertile.
You fill the streams with
    water;
you provide the earth with
    crops.
This is how you do it:
you send abundant rain on the ploughed fields
    and soak them with water;
you soften the soil with showers
    and cause the young plants to grow.
What a rich harvest your goodness provides!

Psalm 65:9–11

We thank you, Great Gardener,
for the little harvests:
for garden raspberries that fill
    a single bowl,
for windfall apples from the
    unpruned tree,
for the one pumpkin in the
    vegetable patch...
From each of these little harvests, we
learn of the miracle of the harvests
that feed us through the year.

All God's creatures

We pray for the wild creatures who fear us;
May we give them space to find safety.

We pray for the wild creatures who make us afraid;
May they give us space to find safety.

We pray for the
world we share
together;
May we and all
your creatures find
a place of safety.

To all the humble
    beasts there be,
To all the birds on
    land and sea,
Great Spirit, sweet
    protection give
That free and happy
    they may live!

*John Galsworthy
(1867–1933)*

He prayeth best, who loveth best
All things both great and small;
For the dear God who loveth us,
He made and loveth all.

Samuel Taylor Coleridge (1772–1834)

Dear God,
May we learn to be gentler towards
flies, midges, mosquitoes, hornets,
bumblebees and wasps.

When I see the birds go soaring,
wheeling, dipping through the sky,
Deep inside my spirit longs to
learn to fly.

Caring for the world

Save me a clean stream, flowing
to unpolluted seas;

lend me the bare earth,
    growing
untamed flowers and
    trees.

May I share safe skies
when I wake, every day,

with birds and
    butterflies?
Grant me a space where
    I can play

with water, rocks, trees, and sand;
lend me forests, rivers, hills, and sea.

Keep me a place in this old land,
somewhere to grow, somewhere to be.

Jane Whittle

Let them all praise the name
   of the Lord!
His name is greater than all others;
   his glory is above earth and
      heaven.
He made his nation strong,
   so that all his people praise him –
   the people of Israel, so dear to him.

Praise the Lord!

Psalm 148

Living for God

Teach me, Lord, the meaning of your
    laws,
    and I will obey them at all times.
    Explain your law to me, and I will obey it;
    I will keep it with all my heart.
    Keep me obedient to your commandments,
    because in them I find happiness.
  Give me the desire to obey your laws rather
    than to get rich.
  Keep me from paying attention to what is
    worthless;
  be good to me, as you have promised.

Psalm 119:33–37

I believe in a God who is strict and fair
Who really knows right from wrong;
I believe in a God who is loyal and kind
Who'll stay with me all my life long.
I believe in a God who enjoys a good joke
Who knows how to laugh and have fun;
Who is planning good times for eternity
When all of my life here is done.

As flowers turn to face the sun,
I turn my life to the light of faith,
the light of hope,
the light of love,
the light of God.

Jesus is born

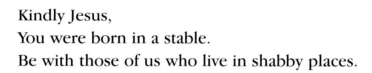

Happy Christmas, God!
Happy birthday, Jesus!
Come to our parties,
come to our feasts,
come to our celebrations,
and let us enjoy being family together.

Kindly Jesus,
You were born in a stable.
Be with those of us who live in shabby places.

You were born on a journey.
Be with those of us who are still searching for a home.

You were given gold and richest gifts.
Be with those of us who have plenty.

You brought the light of heaven to earth.
Bring your light to all of us this Christmas.

'Happy are those who are persecuted because they do what God requires; the Kingdom of heaven belongs to them!

'Happy are you when people insult you and persecute you and tell all kinds of evil lies against you because you are my followers. Be happy and glad, for a great reward is kept for you in heaven.'

Matthew 5:3–12

Jesus said,
'Love your enemies, do good to those who hate you, bless those who curse you, and pray for those who ill-treat you.'

Luke 6:27–28

Jesus said,
'And now I give you a new commandment: love one another. As I have loved you, so you must love one another.'

John 13:34

Prayers of Jesus

Jesus said,
'Ask, and you will
receive; seek, and you
will find; knock, and
the door will be opened
to you.'

Matthew 7:7

Jesus said,
'When you pray, go to
your room, close the
door, and pray to your
Father, who is unseen.
And your Father, who
sees what you do in
private, will reward you.'

Matthew 6:6

The prayer Jesus gave to his followers:

Our Father, who art in heaven,
hallowed be thy name;
thy kingdom come;
thy will be done;
on earth as it is in heaven.
Give us this day our daily bread.
And forgive us our trespasses,
as we forgive those who trespass
against us.
And lead us not into temptation;
but deliver us from evil.

*A traditional version, from
Matthew 6:9–13 and
Luke 11:2–4*

This old ending is often said:

For thine is the kingdom, the power
and the glory, for ever and ever. Amen.

Jesus and the cross

Blessed be the name of Jesus, who died to save us.
Blessed be Jesus, who had compassion on us.
Blessed be Jesus, who suffered loneliness, rejection
    and pain, for our sakes.
Blessed be Jesus, through whose cross I am forgiven.
Lord Jesus, deepen my understanding
    of your suffering and death.

Written by young people in Kenya

Thanks be to thee,
        O Lord Christ,
            for all the benefits which thou hast
                given us;
            for all the pains and insults which
                thou hast borne for us.

O most merciful redeemer,
    friend
    and brother,
    may we know thee more clearly,
    love thee more dearly,
    and follow thee more nearly;
    for thine own sake.

Richard of Chichester (1197–1253)

The autumn leaves were laid to rest
But now the trees are green,
And signs that God brings all to life
        Throughout the world are seen.

And Jesus is alive, they say,
And death is not the end.
We rise again in heaven's light
With Jesus as our friend.

Worshipping God

When the week is at an end,
and the work is done,
let us meet together
with those who love God
that we may say our prayers together
and be encouraged.

The church I like most
has a wide door
and room inside
and a place where I can
   fix my gaze
and think of God;
and there,
when I am quiet inside,
I know that God and I
can hear each other.

When the hours in church are long
May I hear an angel song
Fill my mind with all that's good
Help me live the way I should.

All is silent
In the still and soundless air,
I fervently bow
To my almighty God.

Hsieh Ping-hsin, China

Forgiveness

Forgive
and let live;
mend
and befriend.

Forgive me, God,
Not seven times,
But seventy times
    seven
And seventy times
    seventy
Or I'll not get to
    heaven.

Teach us to forgive
those who do wrong,
and also to work
bravely to prevent
more wrongdoing.

Dear God,
I am not willing to forgive
But I am willing to be made willing…
In just a little while.

God, be merciful to me, a sinner!

Luke 18:13

Dear God,
You gave us a clean new day.
Forgive us all the carelessness that left it messy
   and muddled.
As the sun goes down, help us to make amends
   and make us wiser for tomorrow.

7

AS TWILIGHT FALLS

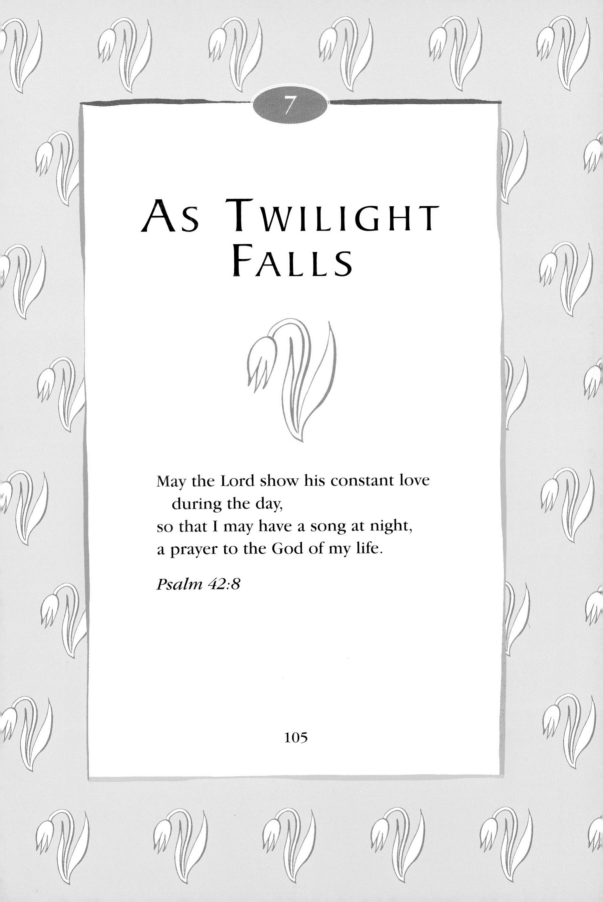

May the Lord show his constant love
  during the day,
so that I may have a song at night,
a prayer to the God of my life.

Psalm 42:8

Unhappy days

Dear God,
When grey thoughts walk behind me
And crowd in round about me,
Shine a light from high above me,
Make a firm path underneath me.

I woke up in the morning
For a bright new day
But then somewhere in the middle
It went wrong.
Now I'm sitting in the gloom
Of a ruined afternoon
And God hasn't sent a miracle along.

The corners of my mouth
just don't want to go up.

Bring me joy when the sky is blue
Hope when the sky is grey.
Comfort me when the clouds are dark
Walk with me each day.

I believe in the sun even when it is not shining
I believe in love where feeling is not
I believe in God even if he is silent.

Inscription on the walls of a cellar in Cologne,
Germany, where Jews hid from the Nazis

Bad news

O God,
The news is bad:
News like a lowering grey cloud;
News like a crushing great load;
News like a deep, dark pit.
O God,
The news is bad.

Dear God,
We pray for people we know who are in distress.
We pray for people in the news who are in distress.
We pray for people who are in distress and who
     feel that no one has noticed.

Let your trouble be,
Light will follow dark:
Though the heaven falls,
You may hear the lark.

Johann Wolfgang von Goethe (1749–1832)

Dear God,
When sadness brings me to tears,
Give me space and time to weep.

As the rain hides the stars,
as the autumn mist hides the hills,
as the clouds veil the blue of the sky,
so the dark happenings of my lot
hide the shining of your face from me.
Yet, if I may hold your hand in the darkness,
it is enough. Since I know that, though
I may stumble in my going, you do not fall.

Gaelic prayer (translated by Alistair MacLean)

Dear God,
Be with me in the dark:
through the night-time dark of shadows;
through the daytime dark of sadness.
Amen.

Feeling ill

I'm feeling so ill,
  I'm feeling so sick.
    Oh, please make me better,
    Oh, please do it quick.

    Dear God, my head is hurting,
      Dear God, my head is sore,
    Dear God, I really don't think
  I can stand it any more.

Dear God, please make me better,
Dear God, be swift to heal,
Dear God, you surely understand
Just how unwell I feel.

Sing praise to the God of the band-aid:
A symbol of wounding, of hurt,
And of love that makes everything better;
Moreover, it keeps out the dirt.

In the darkened room of sickness
Wrap me round with softness
And lay me in a cradle of healing
Where I can sleep till all is well.

8

THROUGH THE NIGHT

All praise to the Lord of the sunset
Who sets the horizon alight
With purples and orange, with red
  and with gold
That smoulder on into the night.

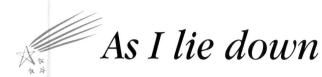

As I lie down

When evening steals the sunshine,
Let me see the golden stars.

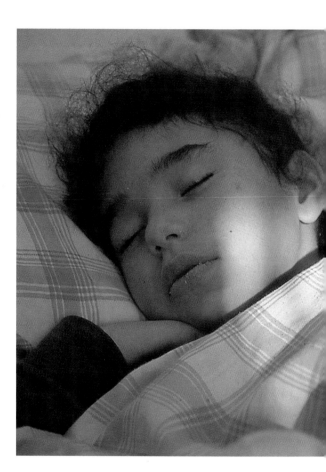

Shadows in the hallway
Shadows on the stair
God be always near me
Everywhere.

When I lie down, I go
to sleep in peace;
you alone, O Lord,
keep me perfectly safe.

Psalm 4:8

The Lord is my light and my salvation;
I will fear no one.
The Lord protects me from all danger;
I will never be afraid.

Psalm 27:1

I climb into my soft bed
and remember those whose life is hard;
I snuggle under my warm quilt
and remember those whose life is cold;
I lay my head upon my pillow
and pray that you will give us all rest.

Who made the night-time
    shadows?
Who made the silver stars?
Who made the moon that
    floats on high
Where clouds and angels are?

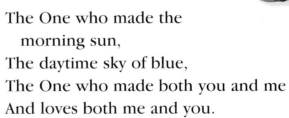

The One who made the
    morning sun,
The daytime sky of blue,
The One who made both you and me
And loves both me and you.

Sophie Piper

Night watch

Watch, dear Lord,
with those who wake,
or watch, or weep tonight,
and give your angels charge
over those who sleep.
Tend your sick ones, O Lord Christ,
rest your weary ones.
Bless your dying ones.
Soothe your suffering ones.
Pity your afflicted ones.
Shield your joyous ones.
And all for your love's sake.

St Augustine of Hippo (354–430)

Dear God,
Wherever the children of your world are at risk
or suffering, please send someone to rescue them:
someone strong and brave who can face the dangers
for them; someone gentle and kind who can make
them feel safe and loved.

Dear God,
Cradle me safely
as my bed floats on a sea of shadows.

I am awake in the night,
and in need of God's help
just like
nurses and doctors,
taxi drivers and truck drivers,
cleaners and bakers,
actors and dancers,
people at noisy parties,
people who weep alone;
those awakened by trains and planes,
disturbed by overloud music
and ill-behaved cats;
those enraged by the clatter of revellers
or the grunts and whistles of snoring;
those in grief because their house is so quiet;
those who count sheep to pass the hours
and those who long to drowse and dream.

119

Blessings

Peace of the running waves to you,
Deep peace of the flowing air to you,
Deep peace of the quiet earth to you,
Deep peace of the shining stars to you,
Deep peace of the shades of night to you,
Moon and stars always giving light to you,
Deep peace of Christ, the Son of Peace, to you.

Traditional Gaelic blessing

Glory to Thee, my God, this night
For all the blessings of the light;
Keep me, O keep me, King of kings,
Beneath Thy own almighty wings.

Bishop T. Ken (1637–1711)

Lord, keep us safe this night,
Secure from all our fears;
May angels guard us while we sleep,
Till morning light appears.

John Leland (1754–1841)

God be with us
On this Thy day,
Amen.

God be with us
On this Thy night,
Amen.

To us and with us,
On this Thy day,
Amen.

To us and with us,
On this Thy night,
Amen.

From Carmina Gadelica

Subject Index

Index of First Lines

125

127